The Road to a College Education

By

Rubye Graham-Emerson

Library of Congress Cataloging in Publication Data 1999

Printed in the United States of America except as permitted under the United States of America Copyright Act of 1997

ISBN: 0-75961-640-X

This book is printed on acid free paper.

Editor: Editorial Services, Inc.
Designer (Text and cover): Wendy Devereaux and LaDana W. Emerson
Research Evaluator of Manuscript: Subhashish DuttaChowdhury

1stBooks - rev. 7/30/01

Acknowledgments

The completion of this project was made possible only through the efforts of many persons. My sincerest thanks and prayers are extended to all of them.

A very special thank you to my entire family: my husband Leroy, my son LeRoy, my daughter LaDana and my grandchildren Dawnavan and LeRoi David. They continue to show me support, patience and unconditional love.

A heartfelt thanks to my daughter, LaDana Emerson, who has served as personal and technical advisor, editor-in-chief, typist and proofreader. You share my love and concern for high school students to continue their education, and you literally worked, on several occasions, until sunup typing and editing. You know I could not have done this without you!

A special thanks to Dr. Jean Prebis, my first instructor, counselor and mentor. You have been both friend and advisor since our first meeting at Purdue University in Calumet, Indiana.

A special thanks to Dr. Byron McKissack, committee advisor, who through his stimulating and challenging classes encouraged me to develop a sensitive spirit of great faith, and to know that "I can do all things through Christ who strengthens me."

A special thanks to Dr. Don Petry, who taught me to appreciate traveling to third world countries and to truly understand that America, although the most blessed nation in the world, is not the only one in the world. You encouraged me to travel with you to Africa, and the experience gave me a real sense of responsibility as well as a new respect for other cultures. It is an experience I shall never forget!

A special thanks to Dr. Larry M. Lindsay for realizing the importance of this material and suggesting I do more than use it as a class project. Your open-mindedness showed me the dramatic difference this material could have on the lives of students and parents who take hold of the vision of higher education.

A special thanks to Johanna Garrison for encouraging me to become a published author. Your support, suggestions and prayers continue to gird me.

A special thanks to Joe Irby, my principal, Faith Christian High School. You encouraged me to attend Oral Roberts University and supported me in continuing my education.

Last, but certainly not least, I want to thank all the students with whom I have had the privilege of working with. Your hunger and focus forced me to examine why expectations are so low for high school students. Faith Christian High School's class of 1998, you are my pride and joy! Valerie Boyskin, Denise Brown, Chris Bryant, Lucille Johnson, Antwan Lison, Brent Meachum, Marcus Miller, Liz Newman, Brandy Rucker, Daniel Steppach,

Andre Vault and Kelli Williams: thank you for allowing me to be your counselor, part-time mom and full-time friend.

Dedication

To my granddaughter, Dawnavan Noelani Emerson, and my grandson, LeRoi David Emerson, may this publication serve as inspiration and guidance to your education goals and future careers.

To my husband, Leroy Emerson, for encouraging me to complete my education goals and continually praying for me and with me everyday. Thank you for logic that was straight, simple and to the point.

To my son, LeRoy Waldo Emerson, for reminding me that seldom did I accept excuses and always did I support and nourish his heart's desires. Thank you for being my voice of reason.

To my daughter, LaDana Wendy Emerson, for reminding me to laugh out loud and who was never too busy to give me input and feedback on my projects. Thank you for being my daughter and my best friend.

Contents

Foreword
By Dr. Larry Lindsay

As an educator I am concerned about the lack of a sense of purpose among parents and students throughout the United States regarding the relationship between a college education and the quality of life. Moreover I am concerned about the lack of understanding among parents about how to get their children admitted to a good college and how little they know about the financial aid opportunities that are available to them. This is especially true among the estimated 15 million "at risk" youth in today's America.

At the Presidents' Summit for America's Future in Philadelphia, several thousand of our nation's leaders endorsed five basic resources that our young people need to become successful adults: (1) a caring adult; (2) safe and structured activities to learn and grow; (3) a healthy start; (4) a marketable skill through effective education; and (5) an opportunity to "give back" through community service (see Appendix B). It is readily noticeable that the family, the school, and the community have shared responsibilities in helping every child realize a healthy quality of life. It is notable, however, that the parents have the first line of responsibility and authority in the process.

Millions of parents and students do not know what they want because they do not know what is available and the preparation that is required when it comes to college admission, financial aid, scholarships, and grants. Rubye Graham-Emerson has identified the critical need for and has captured a vision that will help parents and youth increase their chances for college admission and financial aid. In her book, Rubye has transmitted the inspiration, vision and plan that could enable millions of parents and children seize the opportunities of a college education leading to an improved quality of life. She has shared her heart, mind, research, and success strategies in her booklet for parents and high school students entitled "The Road To A College Education." Rubye's inspirational and informative words are a burning bush calling parents to seize the responsibility for understanding how to support their children in the process of preparing a college resume, seeking admission to college, and for discovering the means of financial aid that can enable their children to enjoy a higher quality of life. This book is must reading for every parent who has questions about what it takes to get into college and how to seek financial assistance in the process.

Professor, Consultant, and Author
Marion, Indiana

1. Introduction

Without realizing what God had in store for me, I began working closely with infants and pre-school aged children in 1965 in hopes of helping them develop a firm foundation of education on which to build. I continued in this field for more than 20 years. Later, I was given the opportunity to work in adult education, specifically with dislocated workers. I recognized at this point that if our junior and senior high school students were not instructed on proper college preparation, a second, third and maybe a fourth generation of skilled laborers would be lost because they would not continue education during their working lives.

Information must be shared with parents and students about the opportunities to attend college through grants, scholarships, fellowships and work-study. The family must understand the importance of early preparation (consistent study habits), good grades and completing applications for funds by the deadlines. The opportunity to obtain a free education, with a present and future (work) position, is highly possible. Most colleges have job fair counseling, on campus, and the students are encouraged to interview with companies for practical experience before graduation.

I think the prophet, Hosea, says it best: "My people (the people of God) are destroyed for a lack of knowledge."

2. Agenda

Recently I had the opportunity to conduct a college preparatory workshop for parents and students of Faith Christian High School. One of the many issues discussed was the availability of funding for attending college—grants, scholarships, fellowships and work-study.

Understanding the importance of early preparation, consistent study habits, good grades and completing applications for the university, and for funds before the deadlines has life-changing ramifications. It is imperative that both the parents and the students realize that delays and excuses almost always lead to the denial of admission, funds or both.

Grant, scholarship and fellowship applications were distributed as examples to help parents and students (first generation) get acquainted with the applications, to lead them step-by-step on how to complete the different ones properly and to become familiar with the necessary support documents for each application (i.e. completed 1040 tax form, essays, samples of work, etc.).

I developed an evaluation form (distributed at the end of the workshop) to receive input from each attendee about the quality of the workshop and the importance of the information provided.

3. Biblically Prepared Handout
(General subjects covered in the workshop)

The workshop was designed to acquaint and prepare students and parents about how to establish a complete plan for attending college. If the student does not receive the necessary preparation, college information, and establish good study habits early in high school, I believe the probability of the student being successful in his/her college career will decrease significantly.

Some significant topics covered in the Preparation for Higher Education (PHE) workshop were: 1) how to complete various applications forms (i.e., college entrance, grants, scholarships, and loan applications), 2) feedback and input from parents and students about what they had learned in the workshop, and 3) how often the workshop should be held.

Understanding:

Trust in the Lord with all your heart, and lean not on your own understanding. In all thy ways acknowledge him, and he shall direct thy path. (Prov 3:5-6)

Preparation:

For which of you, intending to build a tower, sitteth not down first and counteth the cost, whether he have sufficient to finish it? (Luke 14:28)

The soul of the sluggard desireth, and has nothing; but the soul of the diligent shall be made fat. (Prov 13:4)

Study Habits:

Be diligent to present yourself approved to God, a worker who does not need to be ashamed, rightly dividing the word of truth.   (2 Tim 2:15)

Seest thou a man diligent in his business? He shall stand before kings, he shall not stand before mean men. (Prov 22:29)

Diligence:

Go to the ant you sluggard! Consider her ways and be wise. (Prov 6:6)

And it shall be if you diligently obey My commandments which I command you today, to love the Lord your God and serve Him with all your heart and with all your soul. (Deut 11:13)

Student Loans:

The rich ruleth over the poor, and the borrower is the servant to the lender. (Prov 22:7)

He shall lend to thee, and thou shalt not lend to him; he shall be the head and thou shalt be the tail. (Deut 28:44)

Knowledge:

A wise man shall hear, and will increase learning, and a man of understanding shall attain unto wise counsel. (Prov 1:5)

My people are destroyed for the lack of knowledge because thou have rejected knowledge. I will also reject thee, that thou shall be no priest to me; seeing thou hast forgotten the law of God, I will also forget thy children. (Hos 4:6)

Acquaintance:

My son, walk not thou in the way with them. Refrain thy foot from their path; for their feet run to evil, and make haste to shed blood. (Prov 1:15-16)

Be not deceived, evil communication corrupt good manner.   (1 Corin 15:33)

4. Mission Statement and Life Balance Goal

My goal is to assist as many women and young people as I possibly can to achieve their education goals and fulfill their purpose in life. It is essential for all of us to be prepared for the opportunities before they present themselves.

I want to use my life to do God's will. My hope is to encourage, motivate and prepare more students and parents alike to engage in life-long learning. Higher education in today's society is an important key to opening doors of opportunity. We do not embarrass God when we fall down, but we definitely glorify Him when get up and get back in the game!

Spiritual Goals

- Grow in the Lord
- Read and practice God's word
- Pray with individuals immediately
- Listen more and talk less
- Focus on absolute truth

Professional Goals

- Master the computer
- Do more training with parents
- Do "Out of the Box" Thinking
- Encourage more women to return to college
- Work toward completing Doctoral Dissertation

5. Preparation Parents and Students Require

Problem

- How soon should preparation start?
- How soon to start encouraging your children for higher education?
- How does a parent start the process of instilling the necessary values for higher education?
- How is a child encouraged to realize the ultimate goal of graduate studies?

Solution

- Unfortunately, most parents don't realize the importance of emphasizing consistent study habits until it is too late. It is important that the student earn the best possible grades from 9th grade through the 12th grade in order to maintain a high Grade Point Average (GPA). This is the basis for the student's future in terms of receiving grants and scholarships, and ultimately, admission to the college of his/her choice.

- Most ninth grade students are not mature enough to understand how their grades can shape their academic and possibly their professional futures. Therefore, it becomes the duty of the parents to motivate the student, heading him/her in the right direction so that the student develops a habit of achieving good grades. Children are, after all, God's arrows, and the parents are the bows. Parents have

7

to aim children in the right direction so that they grow up to be successful.

- For a better understanding of this, I have included the transcript of a student from Faith Christian High School (see Appendix A). I also have included the American College Test (ACT) scores. As with the example student, note that the ACT score usually improves with each taking of the test.

- The preparation of the high school transcript for college admission begins in the 9th grade, and the student needs to take studies seriously from this point forward. The student must develop consistent study habits and must never lose focus on the ultimate goal in the field of academics. All this depends heavily on how the parents guide the student toward a college education.

- High grades increase the possibility of a student being granted scholarships and loans. It also relieves the parents of the burden of thinking about how to provide for the academic future of their children once they start performing better academically.

Parental Support

- It is evident participation of the parents is as much a factor as that of the student if educational success is to be achieved. Parents should meet and discuss among themselves how they can motivate their children toward a better education future and a desirable quality of life.

- The responsibility to expose students to the ACT, the Preliminary Scholastic Achievement Test (PSAT), the Scholastic Achievement Test (SAT) and the Armed Services Vocational Aptitude Battery (ASVAB) and to conduct the necessary tutoring for these exams lies primarily with the schools. But the interest a parent takes in a child's academic growth and performance has no equal and is the sole responsibility and prerogative of each parent. I hope I have made my point to parents that without their intimate interest in their child's early academic career, the student has little chance for a better education future.

- The bottom line is that it is the parents who can eliminate fear of studying regularly, motivate students, and bring out the best in their own children. This is a message to all the parents who want a bright future for their children. Get to know your children well and motivate the scholar in them to come to the fore. This is one of the prime steps towards a better quality of life for your child.

- Parents need to understand the importance of motivating their child from an early age—much earlier than the 9th grade, because the process of change comes gradually, at best. It does not happen in a day or a week or even a month. The subconscious of a child is highly malleable. Parents can mold the worldview of their child at an extremely early age. The parent has to plant the seed of academic achievement as early as the 5th or 6th grade. Only then is it possible for the child to get into regular study habits and a disciplined lifestyle.

Home Environment

- It is also important to develop an environment in the home of the child that is conducive to studying. A parent must place the child's need to study foremost and sacrifice a bit of social life for this purpose. Often it takes three to four years for a child to become an eager student and start to function as a self-directed learner. This is a crucial period in the life of the child, and if parents neglect the need to aim the child in the right direction, he/she might be distracted from a better education and hence a better life.

Teen-age Relationships

- In the early teens, a new world opens to the student, one of dating, dancing and "being cool." If a parent is impatient about these developments and reacts aggressively, the child usually retreats into a shell and does not respond to any overtures from the parent. Instead, it is wiser to change the parent-child relationship to that of friends and work toward a constructive future. It is always better when a child in his/her early teens feels comfortable discussing any and every issue with parents and mutually satisfactory solutions can be worked out.

The School and Its Responsibilities

- It is also the responsibility of the school to ensure that the child feels comfortable and confident about taking exams that decide his/her future academic career. How can this be achieved? A true and tested solution is at hand. Practice makes one perfect. A child has to be exposed to repeated tests and mental challenges of the kind he/she will face at the crucial stage so that the child can say confidently, "Come what may, I fear only the intangible."

- We know that involvement does matter. As numerous researchers have pointed out (e. g., Astin, 1984; Mallette & Cabrera, 1991; Nora, 1987; Pascarella & Ternzine, 1980; Terenizini & Pascarella, 1977), the greater the student's involvement or integration is in the life of the school, the greater the likelihood that he/she will persist and succeed.

- Inadequate preparation in high school often discourages students from seeking post-secondary education and reduces their chances of achieving higher education degrees (Gillespie, 1998). When there is a positive relationship between the educator's expectation, the student's preparation

11

and the information given, the probability of continuing education is enhanced.

- The high school classroom is at the center of the education activity structure that impacts the student for higher education. The educational encounters that occur there are a major feature in the student's experience. Many college-bound youths underestimate college demands because of open-admission policies, the ready availability of remedial courses, and the failure to prepare adequately for this educational transition. High school students who believe they can make plans for college even if their academic achievement is low tend to reduce their efforts in high school. A 1992 national survey found that while students with low grades can attend college, more than 80 percent of college-planning students with low high school grades have failed to complete any college degree program 10 years later. Studies indicate that high school grades strongly predict education attainment for blacks and whites alike, signifying whether students fulfill their plans, and explaining much of the lower attainment and unrealized plans for disadvantaged students. Although sociologists have produced extensive research showing that grades are related strongly to college attendance (Kerckhoff & Campbell, 1977: Porter, 1974), much of this research is based on study from the 1960s and 1970s. What is the harm in letting students have "high expectations?" Perhaps these plans are just dreams that make students a little happier and do them little harm. This seems to be the belief of some guidance counselors, who say they do not want to disappoint young people. They encourage all students to attend college, even students with low achievement (Rosenbaum, Miller, & Krei, l996). High school grades have proven to be the most influential factor affecting students' failure to attain their original education plans in open-door colleges. This booklet asserts that the best way for community colleges to intervene would be to inform students about what they must do in high school to make their preparation match their education plans. The development of linkage progr- ams between high schools and colleges also may help improve high school students' understanding of college requirements. If this procedure is used, it is possible more students will be encouraged to focus on plans to attend college rather than rationalizing why they cannot be successful there because of their backgrounds or lack of encouragement. These views, however, whether beliefs or rationalizations, are held by 40 percent of students, so they are not just the problems of a few. Indeed, because guidance counselors do not challenge these beliefs, part of the problem arises from school practices (Rosenbaum, Miller & Krei, 1996). The educator should elevate the students' expectations of themselves where education in the formal sense is concerned. For these students, the classroom is the bridge where expectations of proper social beh- avior and academics meet. If positive expectations, early student preparation, and college admission information are going to come together to create a successful college student, it must be in the high school classroom.

- It is evident the high school classroom leaves an impression, whether negative or positive, on the student. The probability of the student continuing to a higher level of education is negative unless more focus on preparation is done at the high school level. The College and Careers Project sought to increase college attendance of at-risk students in the Philadelphia public high schools and to help students link their college and career planning. Students took part in college preparatory classes and career awareness activities throughout the year. Five-week summer internships involved group visits to college campuses, practical experiences in the work world, and exposure to career opportunities. Activities included college application and financial aid workshops; tutoring in science, math, and English; SAT courses, and motivation sessions. Career-related activities included goal setting workshops and presentations by professionals in various fields. Special activities were conducted with students' parents to help them become stronger advocates and provide support for their children in preparing for college and careers. (Fixman, 1993-96). Therefore, while student experiences outside classrooms may have changed, their experiences within them have not.

College Preparation

Activities at school:

Design a college preparation-training program

- This is the master plan to get the maximum number of students inspired to attend college. This plan has to cover everything from parents' responsibilities to building the students' confidence when facing an exam. This plan has to include the most possibilities for addressing problems those students and their parents will encounter along the path of a regular college education.

Plan a college day that involves the entire family

- A day should be designated for each 9th, 10th and 11th grader to invite his/her family to the students school for a college admission workshop. This workshop will afford all the family member the opportunity to be made away of the future possibilities and the right path to follow to achieve a college education. While it is true that most 9th graders and their families will be introduced to the road to be taken to a college education, a different approach should be used with the rest of the students. For those who have been in this session before, it would be worthwhile to review what changes they have undergone individually as a student and collectively, as a family, for getting on the road to success.

15

Conduct a series of parent meetings

- A series of parent meetings is needed. Parents of students must be able to attend an interactive session where they will be able to obtain answers to any questions or issues they have. It is the school's responsibility to make sure the persons presiding at this session are familiar with the information the parents may be seeking. Ideally, the presiding persons would consist of a college recruiter, an official from a student loan organization and a person from the school who can look into the immediate concerns of the parents about current education activities, academic practices and progress of the students.

Develop a student training seminar about how to complete a variety of transcripts and extracurricular activities by deadline

- It is important that both the parents and the students recognize the importance of identifying deadlines and meeting them. The nitty-gritty of completing the transcripts and a variety of financial statements and other forms by the deadline is an exercise with which the parents and the students must be familiar. They are then prepared for the future and are better versed in the process of tackling these issues and completing the documents. It would be a good idea to conduct a workshop in which sample forms are made available from student loan organizations, scholarships, ACT/PSAT/SAT entrance exams and any other relevant documents about future applications regarding college education. Once the parents and students have a "dry-run" experience, they should have a basic idea about how to approach this issue in the future. This workshop can be extended over the deadline period during a second and final meeting. By closely observing each group of parents and students, it will become clear as to how many parents and students could work out the necessary documentation within the given deadline. Dealing with real issues gives a better idea about how to go about handling them. This kind of exercise also brings out practical questions that parents and students could have had earlier, less experienced point.

Conduct tutoring on ACT, PSAT, SAT & ASVAB tests

▪ An entrance examination is a challenge and should be treated accordingly. To say the entrance exam is the student's first impression is not a stretch or an overstatement! Some students fear the very idea or concept of a test. The school is the best institution to wipe out the fear of these tests. The most practical way to do this is to conduct tutoring classes for ACT, PSAT, SAT and ASVAB. Introduce the students to what these exams look like, their contents, and how to achieve good results on them. Children usually have a very objective outlook. If each can be shown that he/she can tackle these exams easily, it will be to their future advantage. Also, emphasis should be put on what the students should practice and how they should go about it. Regularly answering questions and solving problems from sample or earlier tests would work to their advantage, too. Once the students know what they are up against and what to expect, they are a lot more confident than they would be if they had prepared blindly and unsystematically.

Invite military and college recruiters to conduct workshops

- As mentioned earlier, the school should conduct special interactive sessions with the parents, students, college, and military recruiters. Parents and students can ask questions, and recruiters, in turn, can on any topic they are questioned about. It is important parents and students have an idea of what they are about to face in the future. Also, they should hear opinions from the "other side of the table."

- Military recruiters are prepared to offer extraordinary incentives for a student's commitment to active duty or reserve opportunities. Signing bonuses and low-interest college loans can provide enormous financial help for high school graduates.

Focus on parents' needs and concerns

- The staff at school has to address parental needs and concerns and work out solutions to problems they face. Parents have the difficult task of directing their children on the right paths at the time they are moving through different levels of physical and emotional changes. Having a psychologist on hand during such meetings would be advantageous. A psychologist can address, evaluate and give advice on the various concerns and needs of the parents. Also, regular interaction between parents and teachers makes teachers cognizant of the backgrounds and habits of the students, and this helps them handle the children better.

Hold interactive question and answer sessions for students interested in attending college.

- This type of constructive meeting can benefit the students enormously. Most students in high school do not have a distinct idea about what career opportunities are available to them. For example, students may have the impression all engineers work in technical jobs. This is a gross general-ization, and such myths should be destroyed. The students should be made aware that often engin-eers play key roles in management and education fields, sales, and marketing in addition to hard-core technical functions.

- Students also may have a goal in mind but may not know how to achieve it. If a student wants to attend Stanford Management School, he/she must be aware of the fact that to gain admission, the student must possess a Bachelor's degree, have three years of work experience, score high on the

Graduate Management Admission Test (GMAT), and have enough funding to finance the two-year (and very expensive) management education costs.

- The general goal of this meeting is to encourage the students to inquire and get answers to any questions they have about getting on the real road to higher education.

Start communicating the importance of attending college as early as the 9th grade

- One of the most important goals of school authorities should be to communicate the importance of achieving a college education and of readying the students' minds for pursuing this path. This practice should start as early as the 9th grade because the GPA of a student depends on the grades he/she earns from this point through graduation. It just could take that little push from school authorities to get the students on the correct path to higher education. Remember, parents along with the school, are vital to instilling the value of a college education in students. This should begin at an early age and no later than the 9th grade.

It takes four years to prepare for college

- You cannot prepare a student for college in 15 or 30 days, or even in a month or a year. The preparation process is gradual, and the schools have to ease the process into the lives and curriculum of the students. The whole point of this preparation is to have more students prepared to attend college and attain a higher degree of education than at present. In reality, it takes nine years (i.e., 1st-8th grades) to prepare for high school and four years of high school resume building to prepare for college.

Administer practice ACT & PSATs in the 9th, 10th and 11th grades before the students finally take them "for real" in the 12th grade.

- It is important that students are exposed to these exams in the 9th, 10th and 11th grades because the tests are a prerequisite for admission to college. The student's composite score has a chance to increase with each subsequent exam, and when he/she finally present the last score to college for admission purposes, it will be higher than what the student could have achieved then if he/she had appeared only once. It is also a matter of getting accustomed to the idea of taking these exams at least once a year. Once the students know that they can handle the exam, they will face tests with more confidence. When the students finally appear for the exam in the 12th grade, their chances of doing well are quite high.

A Note to School Administrators and Counselors:

- I am sure you are familiar with the rising costs of attending a four-year college. The greatest concern you will face is how much money is available for your present graduating class and how can you help them receive the needed money. On average, 75 percent to 90 percent of the class will want to attend college, and there will be a better possibility this goal will be realized through scholarships and grant programs.

- Faith Christian High School's class of 1997-1998 consisted of 12 students (the sample group). Ten of the 12 students are attending four-year liberal arts colleges, and 9 of the 12 were awarded full or partial scholarships or grants.

Student's "name"	Total Amount Received	University	Scholarships or Grants
Student "1" (female)	$40,800	University of AR at LR	Grant & Scholarships
Student "2" (female)	$31,850	LR Baptist College	Grant & Scholarships
^Student "3" (male)			
Student "4" (female)	$32,512	University of Central AR	Grant & Scholarships
Student "5"(male)	$33,000	Williams Baptist College	Scholarships
*Student "6" (male)		University of AR at LR	
Student "7" (male)	$63,700	Dayton University	Grant & Scholarships
Student "8" (female)	$14,240	Vincennes University	Scholarship
Student "9" (female)	$36,000	Henderson State University	Grants & Scholarship
#Student "10" (male)	– –	School of Worship	(Jerusalem, Israel)
Student "11" (male)	$31,800	Lane College	Scholarship
Student "12" (female)	$16,000	Henderson State University	Scholarship
Total	$299,902		

^Student "3" has a full-time job.

*Student "6" family income exceeded grant and/or scholarship funding levels; however, because the State of Arkansas needs more history teachers, he will be eligible for a three-year scholarship from the History Department (University of AR at LR) if he maintains a 2.0 or C average in this, his freshmen year. The scholarship will net him a total of $12,000.

#Student "10" received funding from family trust allocated for his education by grandparents and other family members.

Rubye Graham-Emerson

Our scholarship/grant program continues to grow each year, netting our students the financial assistance they deserve. The program and workshop I have put together is the sum of my years of experience in working with this on a daily basis. I have seen first hand how well this program works and my prayer is that your school will implement this program and have as much success as we have.

6. An Ethnographic Study

Background

- This study presents the results of multi-method, qualitative and quantitative data as part of a small school reform effort to improve education opportunities for students in Little Rock's neighborhood high schools. The efforts of one private high school as reflected by the class of 1998 could be used as a model for others. Faith Christian High School is being used in this study to illustrate how a school develops student classroom experience through the use of learning communities and through the adoption of collaborative learning strategies. The study seeks to ascertain to what degree such strategies enhance student learning and persistence in focusing on their goals. Beyond its obvious policy implications, the study provides the context for a series of reflections on the ways in which current theories of student persistence might be modified to account more directly for the role of high school classroom experience in the process of both student learning and persistence.

Purpose

- The purpose of this ethnographic study is to observe, describe, and analyze the culture of a private high school as it develops strategies to prepare high school students for college. In what ways do students use the educators' expectations and their own preparation and information to impact their probability of continuing education when they are working independently on their individual plans? The study focuses on factors that could increase the number of African-Americans entering and completing a four-year college education. We will study the success of 36 high school sophomores, juniors and seniors, male and females, who attended a private high school. These students in the classes of 1996, 1997 and 1998 took more than the required number and level of mathematics courses suggested by the administration and were influenced by them. Advanced courses have improved students' chances of going on to college and of completing a Bachelor's degree. The opportunity for advance courses must be available to all students regardless of family income or which school they attend.

Methods

- The research team sampled 10th grade students in the experimental classes and the control classes. We did so first by first selecting a control class and comparison class and then sampling all students in those classes. We did this because the classrooms served as logical units for analysis and because the procedure greatly simplified the task of reaching students. The students were selected from three classes in the Philosophy of Biblical Studies. We used two classes as controls and one sample experimental class that in the view of the program staff, best captured a representative sampling of 10th grade students enrolled in similar subjects but were not enrolled in the control class group. The control class group consisted of students who had no interest in participating or enrolling in a program that would lead them to college preparation. They were focused only on earning credits for high school graduation; continuing their education was not one of their goals.

- Questionnaires were distributed to the experimental and the control group and to the parents of students in both groups at experimental workshops held at the beginning and end of the fall semester. The first workshop introduced the parents to the necessity of preparing their children for college early. The question-naire collected information on a range of student attributes, previous grades, current life situations (e.g., family and work responsibilities), education intentions, parents' education, parents' income, gender, ethnicity, parent's marital status, size of family and attitudes about education. The second questionnaire collected information about how helpful the workshop was in preparing the student for college, out-of classroom activities, estimates of learning gains, why attend a private school, and expectations about completing of high school.

- Measures of student engagement both in and out of the classroom were added to make the mechanical aspects of data analysis more manageable (sorting and retrieving the coded data). The mainframe computer package QUALOG was used. Items were modified to suit the specific context of the institution and program being studied. While ruling out comparisons with previous research, the modifications allowed us to better capture both the intent and impact of program participation on students' behavior.

Theoretical Literature

- The classes of 1996, 1997 and 1998 were asked to describe their high school experiences. The 10th graders discussed a wide range of experiences that required the ability to cope academically and psychologically with the process of growing up and with the sudden increase in college expectations.

- One strategy 'used by educators to help high school sophomores with the transition of preparing for college' is to hold a workshop at which the rules and regulations of attending college are explained. Some students said the workshop and orientation was helpful, and they had no problems finding their classes. Some expressed fears about obtaining enough money for a college education and making the necessary grades to maintain the honors they received while attending high school. Others voiced concerns about extra-curricula activities, a good grade point average, and no social life. The workshop had eliminated some confusion and nervousness about what to expect the first day on campus. Attending college would allow a new level of freedom. College was the key to opening doors to the impressive job positions and would leave a legacy for the generations to come. In confident moments, students felt "grown up and happy" but admitted to feeling they were the pioneers in the family and the problems of the world were on their shoulders. Even under the pressure of peers, they felt that by completing high school and by continuing their education, they were answering their calling with help their preparation in high school and with their "faith" to help carry the load. They did not have time to feel "alone" and "isolated," to experience homesickness, or be fearful about being away from home.

- Most of the experimental sample students in the graduating class of 1998 are attending college now in Arkansas. One student is attending school in Israel and another in Ohio. Students who had friends in high school expressed feeling more initial comfort because they elected to attend the same college. They were able to develop "mature habits in dealing with transitional issues," and felt they became "better people" in the process. They mentioned "confidence" in themselves and saw themselves as changing to exhibit more adult behavior and having more adult interests as a result of their high school preparation. Most were glad that they had been exposed to the workshops in which they had participated in the experimental sample classes. Generally they felt "the classes specifically helped us to deal with stuff by ourselves." All the experimental students are still attending college except the one who was in Israel. The students still in college will give us comprehensive feedback about their education in May 2002. We will then present information about why they stayed in college and finished their education.

Academic

- In addition to providing information about developing the maturity they needed to meet transitional issues, the students responded to questions about their ability to integrate the academic requirements involved in preparing for college. This identified what the student had determined was needed to maintain his role academically and to know the importance his/her being placed in that role. The students discussed their attitudes toward work in high school as well as later in college, the need for time management, and the discipline to be successful in high school that will lead to college success. The concept also included the students' thoughts on their own dedication, motivation, discipline and focus.

- Preparing for college was a common theme, especially for students who were paying their own tuition in a private school. Students expressed an awareness of the importance of "coming to class, doing your work, meeting deadlines and sticking to the program." A few students felt social activities and sports acted as motivators to keep up with the academics because having a common goal with others and being able to socialize, connect and bond increases the inherent desire to remain in that social group, but most students expressed a general desire to do their best. The students in the class of 1998 felt that college courses would be relatively easy because they had been prepared so well in high school, and they had polished their study skills over the last three years. The strat-

egies of the class of 1998 included developing discipline to make themselves do the work, working harder
than they had previously in junior high school (or could
it be no one expected the students to do their best?),
learning how to listen in class, taking notes, reading
material two or three times for deeper understanding,
and using technical equipment to research topics.

- Another important strategy was "making a good sched-
ule," which included studying every night. Time management was particularly important for students who
were commuting, working and involved in extra-
curricular activities.
- The sample included students who were making a
wide range of grades. The students of the class of
1996 maintained a grade point average of 2.15 in high
school. The students of the class of 1997 maintained
an average grade point of 2.25 and the students in the
class of 1998 were the highest achievers, maintaining
a 3.00 GPA on a 4.0 scale. The grade point average in
high school compelled this class to maintain it or
achieve an even higher level to be rewarded with
bonus funds for college.
- Students discussed choosing their classes based on
opportunity to receive a scholarship, grant or fellowship
for college tuition. Most students felt choosing the right
classes was important. They made the effort to attend
each class and to be on time. They sought out faculty
members who expected their students to remain focused.

- The workshop questions dealt with the students' definition of education and their understanding of the importance of education. In their answers, the students shared goals and dreams that included a wide range of subjects from a materialistic viewpoint to the concept that education offers more choices and opportunities to a more intrinsic view of the value of education. Careers such as lawyer, computer analyst, accountant, politician, doctor, banker, engineer, corporate executive and sale managers were popular fields cited in the questionnaires. These were the future career goals of the students from the samples group and every one of the students saw education as the path to reach his/her dream. Most of the students defined education as what they needed to succeed. They defined achieving success as getting a good job or a position of significance that no one in their family ever had held. A good job was defined as one that would offer advancement, good hours, good working conditions, great benefits, and pay a considerable amount of money. Students expressed the desire to be able to provide for themselves and a future family with a standard of living that would encompass "all the things they wanted," such as expensive clothes, money to spend on vacations, large homes and a substantial retirement fund in which they could enjoy after a successful career. The students felt that education would open doors to better careers, a brighter future, and the achievement of goals. Education puts one in the position of being a role model and earning a degree builds character, makes society better, and mentoring others helps them expand their minds, the students said. Remember: students should have a realistic understanding of the requirements to become a lawyer, a doctor, etc. in relation to their GPA.

Conclusions

- I engaged in a qualitative and quantitative study by gathering data during interviews with students, parents and counselors. These are the major conclusions drawn from the findings:

  1. The goals of parents, school counselors and teachers were similar and all were directed toward students who were preparing for admission and success in college. The parents were invited to virtually all of the students' activities, and we sometimes ran special meetings for them conc-urrent with those for the students' (Fixman, 1996).

  2. The students who participated appeared to be focused on their plans after high school and understood the requirements needed to attain their career goals. The experimental group, the class of 1998, was given a file cabinet to prevent lost materials, to track dates of requirements and deadlines, and to demonstrate the importance of each application or form.

Comparison with Other States

"We have discovered that one of the glaring reasons...many of the inner-city students do not do as well as others on standardized tests is that they cannot afford test preparation services,:" revealed T. Willard Fair, president of the Urban League of Greater Miami. "With the College Board's assistance, we're offering those services to our community free of charge. It provides a golden opportunity for us to bridge a void and a gap in access to college preparation," he added.

Fair continued: "We need to get outside the box to connect, prepare, and encourage students. This is a proactive way of helping teachers and students by putting our resources to work at the local level."

We will look at the progress of other states to envision what can be accomplished by following a model plan.

Florida Department of Education:

The Task Force on High School Preparation for Post-Secondary Education and Employment was formed in June 1993. Florida has improved its quality of education by using the Blueprint 2000 plan. If other states adopt the same system, it stands to reason that their educational system may see improvement, as well.

The Task Force was given three charges:

(i) Review high school graduation requirements;

(ii) Make recommendations to the State Board of Education and the Legislature to ensure that students are prepared for post-secondary education and;

(iii) Verify graduation requirements conform to the competency-based goals of the Blueprint 2000 plans.

This report presents the 11-member Task Force's recommendations for:

(i) Raising expectations by making changes in course requirements, focusing on competencies rather than credits, changing grade point average requirements, aligning curriculum and assessment, and making changes in assessment;

(ii) Ensuring a caring learning environment by employing a supportive staff, and development to prepare staff for greater involvement with students and for interdisciplinary and or integrated instruction;

(iii) Providing flexibility for transition to Blueprint 2000 via a modified funding system to support interdisciplinary and/or integrated instruction between vocational and academic courses; and

(iv) Enhancing high school, college, and university collaboration (Castor, 1993).

3. The parents and other family members regularly conveyed high expectations to their children (according to the College and Careers Project: 1993-96). This is a part of the Final Report to the Fund for the Improvement of Post Secondary Education, November 27, 1996. Before participating in the College and Careers project, the majority of parents were, by their own admission, uninformed about the college preparation process even though many of them hoped their children would attend college. As a result of their participation in this project, they said they had become better equipped to motivate their children in the college admissions process. They became knowledgeable about financial aid and scholarships that were available, and they recognized that college was a real option for their children because they saw them talking about it and sharing their aspiration with friends and family.

Most parents saw the need to encourage their children in the college admissions process but were not able to state clearly how they might accomplish this. Most of the parents felt that their children bore the primary responsibility for the college admissions and financing process. When asked how involvement in this project enabled them to help their children make career and college decisions, most focused on the encouragement and motivational aspects. More than one parent became strength-ened in their determination: "I push because I think it is necessary to push. From the time she was knee high, I encouraged her to attend college, not to make it my desire but to make it hers. I see the difference in what's available to people with degrees versus people without them. I don't want my daughter to be sacrificed to welfare, so I push for self-sufficiency"(Fixman, 1996).

Most parents felt college was an option for their children even before they enrolled in this project. What the project provided was an opportunity for parents to support better (and understand) the college admissions process. Parents now engage in frequent discussions with their children about activities in the College and Careers Project, and they have noticed positive changes in their child-ren's interest and performance in school since joining the project. Parents cited increased initiat-ive, a more outspoken demeanor, better grades, and taking school more seriously in their children. Parents perceived their children as having gained a more positive overall attitude toward school, career and college aspirations. Students appeared more interested and focused in their college and career pursuits. As one parent described her daughter: "She has more knowledge of what is available to her"(Fixman, 1996).

Through this project, parents claimed to be less intimidated by the college admission and financial aid processes. They also felt more secure knowing that assistance is available to them through the project and more broadly through the College Access Program. Further, activities and interactions make for more precise communication between parents and students about the college-going process and summer workplace experiences (Fixman, 1996).

4. School-related policies and practices influenced the outcome of the class of 1998. Taking three to four years of advance math coursework, such as algebra II, trigonometry, pre-calculus, and calculus, created self-confidence within the group for college math. A Profile of the American High School Sophomore in 1990, National Education Longitudinal Study of 1988, describes the tested achievement of sophomores in mathematics and patterns of course-taking in mathematics as well as English, science, and social studies. The report summarizes sophomore reports about how they and their families made decisions about school, work, and college plans. Also examined were sophomores' reports on their goals and future plans, including education expectations. Just over 22 percent of the students had achieved the highest level of mathematics mastery, that is, conceptual understanding and complex problem solving. Geometry and foreign language were among the key "gatekeeper" courses for college admission. Overall, gender differences were small, but students did differ in mathematics achievement by socioeconomic status and by high school program placement. While black and white students had similar education expectations, blacks

were much less likely to have studied geometry and foreign languages. Algebra II, trigonometry, pre-calculus and calculus were defined as the advanced math group. The middle-level group comprised those individuals who did not qualify for the advance group but who did report studying one year or more of algebra one or geometry. The low-level math group consisted of all remaining students. (These students had not taken any math or math courses such as general math, business math, and pre-algebra, or less than a year of algebra or geometry). This scheme fits well but imperfectly with the most common ways of sequencing courses in the mathematics curriculum because, in some schools, sophomores may take algebra II before geometry (Ingels, Steven, J and others 1988).

5. The structure of the school environment in these three classes was designed to increase the number of students who took academic classes and the ACT test twice a year. The ACT test usually is required for Southern colleges, but they will accept SAT results for college admission. In designing this project, the College Access Program recognized that students in the Philadelphia neighborhood high schools largely were unaware of the careers for which college could prepare students through testing. Their deliberations about future professions for the most part occurred in isolation from their academic pursuits. In addition, they were attending school in a context that did not focus on college as an expectation for most students.

School District of Philadelphia

Data from the School District of Philadelphia describe a student body generally not prepared well for college. A large number of the city's 52,000 high school student experiences were marked by low achievement.

- Nearly 3 out of 10 students from the 1989 freshman class dropped out before their senior year.

- 49 percent of high school freshmen failed the 9th grade in 1992.

- On the SAT, only two high schools and three middle schools in the District scored above the national average.

- Feeding into the high school, 39 of the 42 middle schools feeding into the high schools ranked below the national norm in reading.

Because these figures include data from the District's selective magnet schools, they do not paint an accurate picture of the 39,000 high school students who attended Philadelphia's neighborhood schools. For the 64 percent African-American, 10.7 percent Latino, 5.1 percent Asian and 29 percent white students whom attended the neighborhood high school last year, the picture is even grimmer. Data from this school district indicate that students are not prepared for college financially or academically.

6. Other peers or friends of students who participated in the study took challenging classes and helped create the expectation that all students should be taking these types of classes, for not only the knowledge obtained but additional benefits.

Rhode Island Department of Education

In 1965, the Rhode Island Department of Education contracted the Big Picture Company to create a "Break-the-Mold" High School to be a model for a statewide effort to improve secondary education. From the beginning, the "Met" co-principals, Dennis Littky and Elliot Washor, envisioned a high school unlike anything seen before. The "break-the-mold" school would hold no formal classes or have school-wide schedules. Students instead would devise their own schedules, consulting with advisors and mentors to develop academic skills as they pursued their interests through authentic work-based experiences. Portfolio exhibitions of student work, as well as student teacher written narratives would supplant grades as the measure of student learning. Parents also would contribute directly to their children's education plans and goals. In September 1996, the "Met" opened its doors to 50 9th grade students. Now a school of 110 students near the end of its second year, the "Met" eventually will house 90 students in nine district schools (Met, 1996).

Finally, it appeared that the synergy created by the interaction of these factors was enough to influence the course selection behavior of 36 students to take academic classes in preparation for college attendance. The findings from the study should begin to fill a void of knowledge while adding understanding that could lead to useful activities in order to persuade more high school educators and students to develop their full potential.

7. Lesson Plan for Parent and Student Workshop

This is a four-week workshop. It is dedicated to preparing the student(s) as well as the parent(s) for college attendance. It is important that the entire family attend the workshop within the preparing student's first year of high school. It is safe to say that technology will continue to develop; therefore, the requirements for college entrance could change. Attending this workshop, or one like it every year, will be a great help in keeping you up-to-date about what is going on.

Course classes will start on the hour and go for 50 minutes with a 10-minute break.

Week One

Day 1 - Monday

Purpose:

Why should you attend college?

- What do you want out of life?
- What can you contribute to society?
- How can you be an example for the next generation?
- What kind of example will you be for your children?
- How much money do you want to earn on your job?
- How long do you plan to work?

Day 2 through 4 – Tuesday through Thursday

Preparation:

How to prepare for college admission:

- Make a list of the college(s) you wish to attend
- Keep in mind the requirements and test scores necessary to be admitted
- Calculate tuition for out-of-state colleges
- Calculate the cost for transportation
- Visit campuses: eCampusTours.com for additional college planning resources, including hundreds of virtual campus tours
- Make appointments to meet with college academic and financial aid counselors
- Check college handbooks for requirement to College Level Examination Program (CLEP) out of freshman courses

(end of week one) Week Two

Days 5 and 1 — Friday and Monday

<u>Calculating College Expenses</u>

- Tuition
- Housing
- Food
- Transportation
- Books and school supplies i.e., pens, pencils, calculator, paper, personal computer, etc.
- Entertainment
- Clothing
- Personal hygiene supplies, etc.

Good study habits must be formed while the student is in junior high school. Join a study group to improve those skills, if necessary. Establishing good study habits early will give you time for more leisure activities or working part time. Parents should not encourage their children to hold part-time jobs the first semester of college. Your student will need time to adjust to the new environment and class load. However, work-study programs are good because work hours are strictly limited and positions are on campus. College counselors will have information on this program.

Parents, encourage your student(s) to get involved in clubs and sports, to do community and volunteer work, and/or to become members in local and nationally recognized organizations. Extra-curricula activities are a part of college admission evaluations.

Parents, discuss financial management strategies with your student. They will need to know how to budget their money and how to apply for a saving and/or checking account. Unless your student is financially mature, credit cards should NOT be given to him/her.

Days 2 through 5 – Tuesday through Friday

Requirements

1. Go through requirements necessary for a four-year college, a two-year college, a vocational college, or a technical college.

Note: permanent records began in the ninth grade

2. Go through pre-entry test requirements
   - How many times each year to take ACT/SAT test
   - How to prepare to take the test
   - What study guides to use
   - How to use computerized practice test

*Students and Parents take entire ACT practice test

3. Go through test requirements
   - How to pre-register for ACT/SAT
   - How much the test costs before the deadline and after the deadline

Note: cost increases after deadline

Note: The composite score on the ACT test results is important. Look at each section to determine if your scores meet the college requirements. (Example: Math 26, English 22, Science 26, etc.)

4. Go through classes necessary to attend a "top 10" college, i.e., math, advance math, trigonometry, physics, calculus, geometry, chemistry and a foreign language.

Week Three

Day 1 and 2 — Monday and Tuesday

5. College admission procedures
    - Complete college admission *application
    - Complete *financial aid applications — parent or parents' federal income tax forms must accompany ALL financial aid applications.
    - Discuss proper attire

Day 3 through 5 — Wednesday through Friday

Low income is not a negative; don't be embarrassed by low income. Quite often lower income may be used as the key to unlocking more college funding. There is money available at little or no interest for those who qualify.

6. Grants and Scholarships
    - What is a grant search
    - How to do a grant search
    - Grant *applications have deadlines
    - Letters from grant searches have deadlines
    - Some nationwide scholarships:
        - Academic Challenge (GPA 2.5-high school)
        - Governor's Scholarship (GPA 3.5-high school)
        - Governor's Distinguished Scholarship (ACT of at least 32 and GPA 3.5-college)

Note: Social Security, childcare and Social Security disability is not considered income.

49

Week Four

Day 1 — Monday

7. Academic Probation in College
   - What is it?
   - How to avoid it
   - Become part of a "mentors" club
   - Be part of a study group (if necessary)

All applications should be typed and not handwritten. It is advisable to practice completing the different kinds of applications before mailing in a final copy!

Days 2 through 5 — Tuesday through Friday

Two days of instruction and two days of guest speakers

Positions:

(Two days of instruction) Check your local library for the top 30 jobs in your state and in the nation. Job rankings vary according to geographical location.

Examples of higher paying jobs:
- Electronic Engineer
- Medical doctor
- Practicing attorney
- Tenured professional at a top 10 university
- Professional athlete
- Certified Public Accountant
- Architect
- Information technology specialist
- Computer network systems specialist

Go through college majors/minors.

"I do not know what I should study in college?" Discussion of: hobbies, interests, motivations, challenges, etc.

Two days of guest speakers

In-Service Presentation Workshop
Feedback Assessment Form

Please evaluate the session you've just attended and the value of the workshop to you on its own merit. Your feedback is very important to us as we strive to meet your training needs. Thank you!

Session   Title

_____

Speaker

_____

	Excellent	Very Good	Good	Average	Fair	Poor
Presentation	7	6	5	4	3	2
Content	7	6	5	4	3	2
Overall Session	7	6	5	4	3	2

Comments:

_____

_____

_____

Name
(Optional)_____

8. What You Must Know Before College

Purpose: Faith Christian High School serves families of students in junior and senior high school. The school is designed to serve 200 students living in Little Rock and the surrounding area. The population consists of multi-culture, low-to-middle income families with a large percentage of single females, heads-of-household. The students come from several cultures: three percent Latin American, two percent Asian American, 32 percent Caucasian and 63 percent African-American.

Statement: To eliminate fear the families must be taught step-by-step how to prepare for the unknown. "Why should I go to college? I can find myself a good job and buy myself a good car. No one else in the family has a college degree. My teacher has a degree and she does not make as much money as my mother." This limited way of thinking must be changed!

Problem: Information must be shared with parents and students about the opportunities to attend college through grants, scholarships, fellowships and work-study. The family needs to understand the importance of early preparation (consistent study habits), good grades and completion of applications for funds before deadline. The opportunity to attain a free education, with a present and future (work) position, is highly possible. Most colleges have job fair counseling on campus, and the students are encouraged to interview before graduation for practical experience.

Rubye Graham-Emerson

Input: "The financial aid application is too hard and I probably won't receive any money, anyway. Most of my friends are not going to college and I am not going to be the first one in my family to go to college and the classes are too hard. Four years is a long time and suppose I fail all my classes. Only one or two people in this neighborhood graduated from college."

Solution:

- Design a college informational training program for parents and students.
- Plan a college day on campus and invite families to attend.
- Hold a series of meetings for the parents.
- Develop a student training seminar on how to complete a variety of college applications, specific essay writings, how to request transcripts and extra-curricula activities by deadline.
- Conduct tutoring on ACT, PSAT, SAT & ASVAB tests.
- Invite military and college recruiters to conduct workshops.
- Focus on parental needs and concerns.
- Hold meetings for students interested in college that include question and answer session.
- Start communicating the importance of attending college as early as 9th grade.
- Teach specifically on "It takes four years to prepare for college."
- Administer ACT, SAT or PSAT for 9th, 10th and 11th graders.

Choice:

- Giving more attention to strengths and weakness. Changes can be made in areas of unwanted desires in which the students are not acquainted. "Yes, you

cast off fear" (Job 15:4)   "Whom (what) shall I fear"
(Ps 27:1) and "Be strong, do not fear" (Is 35:4).

- Information given years before going to college will increase knowledge and desires.   "Knowledge is wisdom" (Ecc 7:12); "Knowledge shall increase" (Dan 12:4) and "More accurate knowledge" (Acts 24:22).

- Students without stable homes, who bond with positive role models, have a better chance of achieving goals. "Share in all good things" (Gal 6:6) "Now no chastening seems to be joyful for the present, but painful; nevertheless, after way it yields the peaceable fruit of righteousness to those who have been trained by it" (Heb 2:11).

Operation Goal (Action Steps):

- Eliminate parental and the students' excuses
- Parents and students understanding is clear
- Deadlines are met
- Packages of information showing step-by-step procedures
- Team work development
- Goals are clear
- Increase relationships
- Assignments are understood
- Recruit mentors
- Remove all doubts

Suggested Steps in Applying for Financial Aid:

1) CONTACT: Contact each school you are interested in attending.

   a.) You need to contact <u>both</u> the Admissions and Financial Aid Offices (sometimes referred to as the Student Aid Office). Do not confuse the <u>ADMISSION</u> process with the <u>FINANCIAL AID</u> process.

   i. Request an application for admission, a catalog, and financial aid applications. Be sure which academic year you plan to attend (e.g. 1999-2000). If you are interested in scholarships, request information specifically about scholarships and scholarship application forms.

   ii. Read the information sent to you. Be familiar with the admission requirements. Make sure the school can offer you the type of degree you want.

   b.) DEADLINES: Make sure you are aware of the Admission and Financial Aid deadlines. <u>APPLY EARLY</u>! Some Financial Aid deadlines are as early as February 1 for the next academic year. Some colleges offer special scholarship to students who are classified as JUNIORS in high school.

2) Find out what applications are required for financial aid.

    a.) Analysis: required for Free Application for Student Federal Student Aid (FAFSA).

    b.) Institution Application: required by most schools. Usually asks general information (e.g. name, social security no., permanent address etc).

    c.) Scholarship application:

        i.   Usually requires three letters of recommendation (LOR). Good sources for LOR are high school counselors, teachers, high school principals, pastors and/or employers.

        ii. Do a dry run. Complete an application in pencil first to ensure neat penmanship. Make sure all final applications are completed thoroughly. Handprint in dark inks (black or black-blue) or use a typewriter.

    d.) Loan Application: always required if the student is applying for an educational loan.

    e.) Other forms may be required as application process progresses. Ask which forms are required to have a completed financial aid application.

FINANCIAL AID PROCESSING

STEPS   COMPLETED

- Priority Deadline date _____   _____
- Campus financial aid forms requested   _____
- Scholarship information requested   _____
- Financial need analysis packet obtained   _____
  (FAF, FFS, USAF Single File, ASFA)
- Need analysis mailed   _____
- Student Aid report mailed to college   _____
- Scholarship applications submitted   _____
- Verifications documents (income tax)
  Submitted   _____

STUDENT HOUSING

STEPS   COMPLETED

- Housing deadline date   _____
- Housing application requested   _____
- Application mailed   _____
- Housing deposit mailed   _____

The above can be used as a checklist to ensure all necessary forms have been submitted to the proper agencies and organizations by the deadlines.

9. What to Consider in Selecting a College

ADMISSION CRITERIA

- **Intended Major:** Is the student clear about what major he/she wants? What does the future hold for a person who graduates with the major the student wants to study? All this information has to be obtained in advance by the students and parents before deciding on a major.

- ***Essay:*** The essay that states why the student wants to enroll at that particular college and why the student is interested in a particular major has to be written with heartfelt conviction. It must be strong enough to persuade the person reading it to accept the student. A good move would be for the student to write the essay and get the opinion of his/her parents and school counselors. Remember, Admission and Scholarship boards look for students who are well-rounded and show evidence of being involved in extra-curricula activities, such as school clubs, sports, volunteer service, and church groups. These groups also look for students who have held a part-time job.

- **Minority Status:** If you qualify for a minority status, be sure to be aware of the benefits stemming from that particular qualification.

- **High School Course Work:** For getting into college, students should take courses such as advanced math, calculus, etc. Students also should take advance level science courses, such as biology, chemistry, and zoology. These advanced classes will make students better prepared for taking similar college-level courses. This facilitates not only admission to good colleges but also financial aid, grants, and scholarships. Parents also should be aware of the advanced courses their children are required to "master" for college acceptance. Students should have a good idea about what they are going to face in terms of number of hours of study in school and the hours they are expected to spend on homework. They should have an idea as well of the extra-curricular activities and sports opportunities available in the college they are about to attend.

- **Class Rank:** The student should try to be in the top 25 percent of the class. This helps when the student is on his/her own because it demonstrates drive and direction to perform well consistently.

- **Grade Point Average:** Grade Point Average is one of the most vital criterions to gain acceptance in the college of one's choice. A GPA of 3.5 or higher is desirable.

- **Activities:** Both students and parents need to be aware of the curricular and extra-curricular activities that a student needs to and in which he/she can participate in college. The parents and the authorities should not encourage sports activities and gym participation.

- **National Test scores:** It is important to monitor continuously how the student has rated in National Test Scores such as Stanford Testing and the usual PSAT, ACT, SAT or ASVAB. Acceptance to a college of one's choice often depends on these scores.

  - Completed admissions package requirements
  - Achievement results – are they required?
  - Open admissions policy or selective admissions policy?
  - Early decision date
  - Admissions application deadline
  - Campus visit eCampusTours.com

Housing

- Have you visited the dormitories?
- Room appearance
- Air conditioning
- Meal plan – 15, 18 or 20 meals a week
- Application deadline date
- Application fee
- Reservation fee
- One-year advance selection

- Housing application with or without admission application?
- Move-in dates and move-out dates

Registration and Advising

- Required orientations
- Student-parent orientations
- Faculty advising dates
- Registration dates
- Advance placement or challenge testing dates and processes
- College or parent assistance for registration

Tuition payment plans

- One-time payment
- Deferred payment
- Prepayment
- Installment payment

Rubye Graham-Emerson

Miscellaneous

- Student health insurance/family health insurance
- Local physician
- How close are stores and malls
- Automobile registration and cost
- Personal expense money

Packing

- What do I take and what do I need?
- How much room do I have?
- Start-off supplies needed on arrival

What Does It Cost To Attend the College of Your Choice?

I have chosen four well-known Christian and non-Christian universities for this example. Often parents and students are not aware of the "hidden costs" of attending a university. The figures listed below for the University of Dayton in Dayton, Ohio, and Williams Baptist College in Walnut Ridge, Arkansas, include tuition and housing. However, the figures listed below for Oral Roberts University in Tulsa, Oklahoma, and the University of Arkansas at Little Rock in Little Rock, Arkansas is **tuition only**! (This is one reason more workshops and pre-college conferences should be held in high schools!)

Oral Roberts University	4 years undergraduate program	$40,000*
University of Arkansas at LR	4 years undergraduate program	$16,000*
Williams Baptist College	4 years undergraduate program	$24,000*
University of Dayton	4 years undergraduate program	$65,000*

* - Cost of tuition in 1998. Tuition cost is subject to change.

TOP 30 OCCUPATIONS IN ARKANSAS

The information below was gathered from the Arkansas Occupational Information System. Titles were ranked based on projections of the average annual growth rate from 1996-2005.

Provided by Student Outreach Services
A service provided by
Educational Services of America, Inc. (edamerica)

Top 30 Positions	Annual Growth Rate	Average Job Openings
1. Personal and Home Care Aides	13.7%	185
2. Home Health Aides	12.2%	715
3. Residential Counselors	10.6%	255
4. Computer Engineers	10.1%	165
5. All Other Computer Scientists	9.7%	95
6. Teachers, Preschool and Kindergarten	9.5%	495
7. Systems Analysts, Electronic Data Processing	9.3%	710
8. Physical and Corrective Therapy	8.4%	155
9. Physical Therapists	8.2%	160
10. Computer Support Specialists	7.8%	70
11. Occupational Therapists	7.6%	60
12. Manicurists	7.2%	50
13. Machine Builders & Other Precision Machine Assemblers	6.8%	130
14. Operations & Systems Researcher/ Analysts, Except Comp	6.7%	55

15.	Human Services Workers	6.5%	145
16.	Child Care Workers	6.4%	1035
17.	Nursery Workers	6.4%	105
18.	Paralegal Personnel	6.3%	75
19.	Medical Assistants	6.3%	305
20.	Numerical Control Machine Tool Operators and Tenders	6.3%	70
21.	Medical Records Technician	6.2%	110
22.	Combination Machine Tool Setters and Set-Up Operators	6.2%	100
23.	Speech and Language Pathologists and Audiologists	5.9%	80
24.	Geologists, Geophysicists, and Oceanographers	5.8%	35
25.	Teachers, Special Education	5.7%	395
26.	Emergency Medical Technicians	5.7%	175
27.	Detectives and Investigators, Except Public	5.6%	40
28.	All Other Precision Assemblers	5.6%	30
29.	Surveyors and Mapping Scientists	5.4%	35
30.	Bus Drivers, Except School	5.4%	145

TOP 30 OCCUPATIONS IN THE U. S. A.

The information below was gathered from the U. S. Bureau of Labor Statistics. Titles were ranked based on projections of the average annual growth rate from 1996-2006.

Provided by Student Outreach Services
A service provided by
Educational Services of America, Inc. (edamerica)

Top 30 Positions	Annual Growth Rate	Average Job Openings
1. Database Administrators, Computer Support Specialists and All Other Computer Scientists	11.8%	24900
2. Computer Engineers	10.9%	23500
3. Systems Analysts	10.3%	52000
4. Personal and Home Care Aides	8.5%	17100
5. Physical and Corrective Therapy Assistants and Aides	7.9%	6600
6. Home Health Aides	7.7%	37800
7. Medical Assistants	7.4%	16600
8. Desktop Publishing Specialists	7.4%	2200
9. Physical Therapists	7.1%	8100
10. Occupational Therapy Assistants and Aides	6.9%	1100
11. Paralegal	6.8%	7600
12. Occupational Therapists	6.6%	3800
13. Teachers & Special Education	5.9%	24100
14. Human Services Workers	5.5%	9800
15. Data Processing Equipment Repairers	5.2%	4200
16. Medical Records Technicians	5.1%	4400
17. Speech-Language		

	Pathologists and Audiologists	5.1%	4400
18.	Dental Hygienists	4.8%	7700
19.	Amusement &		
	Recreation Attendants	4.8%	13800
20.	Physician Assistants	4.7%	3000
21.	Respiratory Therapists	4.6%	3700
22.	Adjustment Clerks	4.6%	18300
23.	Engineering, Science		
	& Computer Systems Manager	4.5%	15500
24.	Emergency Medical Technicians	4.5%	6700
25.	Manicurists	4.5%	1900
26.	Bill & Account Collectors	4.2%	11200
27.	Residential Counselors	4.1%	7400
28.	Instructors & Coaches,		
	Sports and Physical Training	4.1%	12300
29.	Securities & Financial		
	Services Sales Workers	3.8%	10000
30.	Dental Assistants	3.8%	7700

10. Internet Resources

Harnessing the power of the Internet to obtain the information available on the World Wide Web is a good starting point for both students and parents. You can have advance information about admission and acceptance criteria, and residential, sports and gym facilities on and around the campus. Another important aspect to monitor over the Web is the availability of part-time on-campus or off-campus jobs.

The most viable subject to look for on the web is scholarships and grants. For this reason, I have listed some web sites that you can browse for information. Also, there are sites dedicated to financial aid for students.

Almost all the colleges have web-sites that list various cost, including tuition, housing, and transportation. Additional information can be obtained by e-mailing the appropriate person(s) at the college(s). Information about assistantships and part-time jobs usually is listed on the college web site also.

Web Sites for Scholarships:

http://www.edsouth.org
*An extensive site with information on the basics of financing a college education. Conduct free scholarship searches and view information on choosing a career. Learn about a variety of student loans for parents, undergraduate & graduate students - including federal Stafford, PLUS (parent) private and consolidation loan programs. This site is jammed packed with superb information!

http://www.scholarships.com
Has a comprehensive search that enables you to find exactly what you're seeking…an excellent site.

http://www.fastweb.com
Free Scholarship and College Searches and Financial Aid Tools.

http://www.muhlenberg.edu/library/ref/acad
Grants and Scholarships. A catalog of federal domestic assistance containing a directory of all grant opportunities sponsored by the federal government.

http://www.ncsu.edu/provost/governance/standingcommitt ees/SSAC
http://www.ncsu.edu/provost/governance/standing committees/SSAC
University Standing Committee on Scholarships and Student Aid. 1999-2000.

Rubye Graham-Emerson

http://www.floridalink.com/thenews/collegegrants.htm
Florida College Grant Guide and College Grant Links.

http://www.collegeboard.com
College Board on the web.

11. General Grant Information

1. Governor's Scholarships Programs (includes Governor's Distinguished Scholars in Arkansas). Available at your state governor's office.

2. Robert C. Byrd Honors Scholarship: Available at your state Department of Education office.

3. Arkansas Academic Challenge: Available at Arkansas Department of Higher Education (ADHE), 114 E. Capitol Avenue, Little Rock, Arkansas, 72201. *Restricted to high school graduates with specified GPAs and family income limits. Also deadline sensitive.*

4. U.S.A. Group Scholarship: Available at your local high school counselor's office.

5. 2000 Imagine American Scholarship: Available at your local high school counselor's office. *Limited to Year 2000 high school graduates who were enrolled in a college or university by June 1, 2000.*

6. Federal Grain Inspection Service (FGIS) Scholarship Program. Call 1-800-762-2738 to obtain application.

7. Burger King McLamore Youth Opportunities Foundation. *The first scholarship awards were made in April 2000. High school principals nominate students, and a selection committee of professional educators selects the winners of the BURGER KING FOUNDER'S AWARD each spring.*

12. College Level Examination Program

College Level Examination Program (CLEP) is a national program through which students may obtain college credit in certain subjects by making certain scores on comprehensive examinations. *Score requirements may vary with each college. Check with your counselor or admissions specialist for details.*

"Testing out" refers to receiving college credit by making an acceptable score on a comprehensive test in a certain subject or discipline. A major Arkansas university offers such tests in two ways: those designed by the University and those designed by national programs such as CLEP. There often is a fee for the tests. *Contact the Office of Admissions and/or the handbook of the college you will attend under TESTING-OUT or CLEP.*

13. Demographics from a Study

(Class of 96)

Gender	Ethnicity	College	Family	Parent Income Education
Male	Black	U of AR @ LR	$15-$18K	Non-degree
Female	White	U of MS @ Jackson	$35-$45K	Non-degree
Male	Black	No	$28-$30K	Non-degree
Female	Black	Drop-out	$40-$50K	Non-degree
Female	Black	Drop-out	$17-$20K	Non-degree
Male	Black	Drop-out	$100-$120K	Degree
Male	Black	No	$15- $18K	Non-degree
Female	Black	Drop-out	$18-$20K	Non-degree
Female	Black	No	$18-$20K	Degree
Male	Black	U of AR @ LR	$19-$21K	Non-degree
Male	Black	No	$75-$100K	Non-degree
Male	Black	No	$17-$	Non-degree
Male	Black	No	$20-$25K	Non-degree

(Class of 97)

Gender	Ethnicity	College	Family	Parent Income Education
Female	Black	Henderson State	$30-$35K	Non-degree
Female	Black	U of AR @ LR	$50-$65K	Non-degree
Male	Black	No	$18-$20K	Non-degree
Female	Black	Drop-out	$15-$18K	Non-degree
Male	Black	No	$25-$35K	Degree
Female	Black	Ouachita State	$125-$150K	Degree
Female	Black	U of AR @ LR	$60-$75K	Degree
Male	Black	No	$50-$60K	Non-degree
Female	White	U of AR @ LR	$50-$55K	Degree
Female	Black	U of AR @ LR	$45-$55K	Non-degree
Male	Black	No	$50-$60K	Degree
Female	White	No	$50-$65K	Non-degree
Male	Black	No	$50-$65K	Degree

(Class of 98)

Gender	Ethnicity	College	Family	Parent Income Education
Female	Black	U of AR @ LR	$15-$18K	Non-degree
Female	Black	AR Baptist	$30-$40K	Non-degree
Male	Black	No	$20-$25K	Non-degree
Female	Black	U of Central AR	$20-$30K	Non-degree
Male	Black	Baptist College	$30-$50K	Non-degree
Male	White	No	$75-$100K	Non-degree
Male	Black	Univ. of Dayton	$30-$35K	Non-degree
Female	Black/White		$75-$100K	Degree
Female	Black	Henderson State	$28-$35K	Non-degree
Male	White	Israel	$150-$175K	Degree
Male	Black	U of AR @ LR	$20-$25K	Degree
Female	Black	Henderson State	$25-$30K	Non-degree

76

14. References

Astin A., (1984). Mallette & Cabrera, (1991). Nora, (1987). Pascarella & Terenzine, (1980). Terenzine & Pascarella, (1977). "Classrooms as Communities." *Journal of Higher Education.* Vol. 68, No. 6. Abstract from The ERIC Document Reproduction Service: ERIC.

Castor, B. (1993). "Recommendations for High School Preparation for Post Secondary Education and Employment." Report to the Florida State Board of Education by the Task Force on High School Preparation for Post Secondary Education and Employment. Abstract from THE ERIC Database; ERIC Item: ED 370633.

Fixman, C.S. (1996). "College and Careers Project." Abstract from THE ERIC Database; ERIC Item: ED 417624.

Gillispie, M.D. (November 1998). "Comparison of Academic success variables of black male high school graduates with other racial and gender populations in the Broward County School District, Florida." *Dissertation Abstracts Online, 59- 02A.* (Doctoral dissertation, Florida Atlantic University, 1998).

Ingels, S.J.; Plank, S.B.; Schneider, B. and Scott, L.S. (1994). "A Profile of the American High School Sophomore in 1990." *National Education Longitudinal Study of 1998.* Abstract from THE ERIC Database; ERIC Item: ED 380515.

Kerckhoff, A.C. and Campbell, R.T. (1977). "Black differences in educational attainment process." *Sociology of Education.* 50 (11). 15-27 Kerckhoff & Campbell (1977); Porter (1974). "The Philadelphia Partnership: Improving College Access and Retention Among Minority and Low- Income Students." Abstract from THE ERIC Database; ERIC Item: EJ 573801.

Kruis, John G. *Quick Scripture References for Counseling.* (Michigan: Baker Books, 1995); pp. 1-140.

Rosenbaum, J. (1998). "Unrealistic Plans and Misdirected Efforts: Are Community Colleges Getting the Right Message to High School Students?" Community College Research Center Occasional Proper. Abstract from THE ERIC Database; ERIC Item: ED 428795.

Rosenbaum, Miller & Krei (1996). "The Philadelphia Partnership: Improving College Access and Retention Among Minority and Low-Income Students." Abstract from THE ERIC Database; ERIC Item: EJ 573801.

Endorsements

Arkansas Governor Mike Huckabee said of *The Road to A College Education*: "As I helped pack the last of my three children off to college in the fall of 2000, I was realizing that getting ready for college is a family affair— the student has to choose the school, the course of study, and a roommate, but the parents have to think about how to afford it and cope with the 'departure' of that special gift from God who is moving out for more than a summer camp. My friend, Rubye Graham-Emerson, has prepared a simple yet helpful book that gives some driving tips along *The Road to A College Education.* I hope you'll enjoy the trip!"

"Ruby Graham-Emerson has dedicated herself to young people. Her book, *The Road to A College Education*, is but one product of that dedication. This book provides the practical information needed to equip parents, teachers, counselors, pastors and youth workers in their work of providing hope for and a plan for higher education. I recommend it to you. **U.S. Senator Y. Tim Hutchinson**, (R-Ark.)

"Isn't it ironic that self-sufficiency originally starts with support from others? This book does a wonderful job proving that point as it explores the important roles parents, the home environment, the schools and even the Bible have in relation to getting an education. It is truly refreshing to see how the author expounds on the Biblical perceptiveness of pursuing an education. I strongly believe that helping students get the proper state of mind is key to creating an atmosphere conducive to learning. It is encouraging to see that someone of Rubye's insight would care enough about students to write this type of helpful material—material that explores the behind the scenes type of information they need to know. This book will be a benefit for students from all backgrounds as they journey through the educational process. **Dr. Alton Garrison**, Senior Pastor, First Assembly of God, North Little Rock, Arkansas.

Author **Johanna Garrison** on *The Road to A College Education*: "If you want a crash course in getting a college education, buy this book! Rubye's advice is sincere and heartfelt. In a very practical yet helpful way, it reveals: how to save money, how to get into a top college, and facts on choosing a field of study that is in demand within the state and around the country. The author also shares helpful resources from the Internet as well as excellent references from the education community. This is a good resource for any parents looking to help their child or for an older student who is going back to college. I wish this type of book had been around before I entered college."

Rubye Graham-Emerson's book, *The Road to A College Education*, is filled with practical tools and sound research- based information that is a must have for all parents. Packed with helpful suggestions, this book could serve well as the road map for all families wanting their children to achieve their fullest potential and attend a college of their choice. *The Road to A College Education* provides a practical, step-by- step guide for planning and determining your options for attending the top colleges. Thank you, Rubye, for your valuable insight and dedic- ation to helping all young people achieve their greatest dream. **Ms. Cynthia Klumpp,** Arkansas Promise Coordinator.

"This book serves as a valueble tool to both students and parents who are interested in exploring the educational Financial Aid process. It is a well-researched resource that genuinely reaches out to students and families of all social and economic backgrounds."

Wm. Anthony Hollin
Chairman/CEO
Edmerica
Edorsement

Rubye Graham-Emerson

Order Form

Item No.	Name of Item	Quantity	Price	Total
#DL12	The Road to a College Education (Book)		$12.99	$
#DL13	Preparation for Higher Education (PHE) Workshop	1-99 students 99+ students	$300.00 $3.00 per	
#DL 14	PHE Workshop Material		$3.00 per	$
SORRY NO C.O.D.'S		Add 10% For S/H		$
				$
				$
			Total	$

Please Print

Name: _____

Address: _____

City: _____

State: _____

Daytime Phone: _____

____ Check _____ Money Order _____ Visa

____ MasterCard _____ AMEX

Signature _____

Card # _____ Expiration Date _____

Mail to: **Rubye Emerson** *4808 W. 30th St. Little Rock, AR 72204*

Workshop Information

_____ I would like more information on Preparation for Higher Education Workshop.

_____ I would like a Preparation for Higher Education Workshop conducted at my educational facility.

Please Print

Name: _____

Address: _____

City: _____

State: _____

Daytime Phone: _____

____ Check _____ Money Order

____ Visa _____ MasterCard _____ AMEX

Signature _____

Card # _____ Expiration Date_____

*Mail to: **Rubye Emerson** 4808 W. 30th St. Little Rock, AR 72204*

Appendix A
Faith Christian High School Student's Transcript

Faith Christian High School
6111 West 83rd Street
Little Rock, AR 72209

OFFICIAL TRANSCRIPT
School Phone: (501) 568-3247
Page: 2

SOC. SEC. NO.:
Transcript continued for:

Year	Term	In-House	Class Name	Grade	Credits Attempt	Earn
1997-1998	1ST	Yes	Advanced Math (Geom/Trig)	93	0.500	0.500
1997-1998	1ST	Yes	Church History/Christian	95	0.500	0.500
1997-1998	1ST	Yes	Computer II	87	0.500	0.500
1997-1998	1ST	Yes	English 12	95	0.500	0.500
1997-1998	1ST	Yes	Government And Economics	93	0.500	0.500
1997-1998	1ST	Yes	Health	90	0.500	0.500
1997-1998	1ST	Yes	Spanish II	98	0.500	0.500

GPA: 3.8571   Total Credits: 3.500   3.500

Year	Term	In-House	Class Name	Grade	Attempt	Earn
1997-1998	2ND	Yes	Advanced Math (Geom/Trig)	97	0.500	0.500
1997-1998	2ND	Yes	Brush Art	94	0.500	0.500
1997-1998	2ND	Yes	Church History/Christian	79	0.500	0.500
1997-1998	2ND	Yes	Computer II	97	0.500	0.500
1997-1998	2ND	Yes	English 12	95	0.500	0.500
1997-1998	2ND	Yes	Government And Economics	85	0.500	0.500
1997-1998	2ND	Yes	Spanish II	100	0.500	0.500

GPA: 3.5714   Total Credits: 3.500   3.500

Cum. GPA: 3.5385   Total Cum. Credits: 26.000   26.000

ACT SCORES

Date	English	Mathematics	Reading	Sci. Reas	Composite
12/22/1996	13	16	11	16	14
Subscores:	5 7	8 7 8	5 4	% At/Below Nat. Comp.: 8	

Date	English	Mathematics	Reading	Sci. Reas	Composite
04/20/1997	15	14	13	16	15
Subscores:	7 8	7 5 6	5 8	% At/Below Nat. Comp.: 13	

Date	English	Mathematics	Reading	Sci. Reas	Composite
10/25/1997	18	16	14	20	17
Subscores:	10 9	8 9	6 8	% At/Below Nat. Comp.: 26	

Date	English	Mathematics	Reading	Sci. Reas	Composite
04/11/1998	17	16	16	14	16
Subscores:	8 9	10 4 8	9 6	% At/Below Nat. Comp.: 19	

Comments:

1995-1996: Basketball
1996-1997: Spanish Award; Volleyball
1997-1998: F.B.L.A.   ; Yearbook Staff
* *

Authorized Signature: _Joseph Daly_ _____

84

The Road to a College Education

Faith Christian High School
6111 West 83rd Street
Little Rock, AR 72209

OFFICIAL TRANSCRIPT
School Phone: (501) 568-3247
Page: 1

NAME: PHONE: DATE: 06/19/2000
                                               SOC. SEC. NO.:   GENDER:
          LITTLE ROCK, AR   DATE OF BIRTH: ENROLLED:
                                               GRADUATED: 05/28/1998

| | | | | | Credits | |
Year	Term	In-House	Class Name	Grade	Attempt	Earn
1994-1995	1ST	No	Algebra I	A	0.500	0.500
1994-1995	1ST	No	Bible Senior Girls	A	0.500	0.500
1994-1995	1ST	No	Biology	B	0.500	0.500
1994-1995	1ST	No	English 9	B	0.500	0.500
1994-1995	1ST	No	P.E.	A	0.500	0.500
1994-1995	1ST	No	World History	B	0.500	0.500

GPA: 3.5000   Total Credits: 3.000   3.000

1994-1995	2ND	No	Algebra I	A	0.500	0.500
1994-1995	2ND	No	Bible Senior Girls	A	0.500	0.500
1994-1995	2ND	No	Biology	C	0.500	0.500
1994-1995	2ND	No	Choir	A	0.500	0.500
1994-1995	2ND	No	English 9	B	0.500	0.500
1994-1995	2ND	No	World History	B	0.500	0.500

GPA: 3.3333   Total Credits: 3.000   3.000

1995-1996	1ST	No	American History	A	0.500	0.500
1995-1996	1ST	No	English 10	B	0.500	0.500
1995-1996	1ST	No	Fd & Ntr: Sem	A	0.500	0.500
1995-1996	1ST	No	Geometry	B	0.500	0.500
1995-1996	1ST	No	Science/Tech	A	0.500	0.500
1995-1996	1ST	No	Spanish I	B	0.500	0.500

GPA: 3.5000   Total Credits: 3.000   3.000

1995-1996	2ND	No	American History	B	0.500	0.500
1995-1996	2ND	No	Cl & Tex: Sem	A	0.500	0.500
1995-1996	2ND	No	English 10	B	0.500	0.500
1995-1996	2ND	No	Geometry	B	0.500	0.500
1995-1996	2ND	No	Science/Tech	A	0.500	0.500
1995-1996	2ND	No	Spanish	A	0.500	0.500

GPA: 3.5000   Total Credits: 3.000   3.000

1996-1997	1ST	Yes	Algebra II	97	0.500	0.500
1996-1997	1ST	Yes	Chemistry	99	0.500	0.500
1996-1997	1ST	Yes	Computer I	88	0.500	0.500
1996-1997	1ST	Yes	English 11	86	0.500	0.500
1996-1997	1ST	Yes	Geography	86	0.500	0.500
1996-1997	1ST	Yes	History/Writings Of Early	85	0.500	0.500
1996-1997	1ST	Yes	Spanish I	99	0.500	0.500

GPA: 3.4286   Total Credits: 3.500   3.500

1996-1997	2ND	Yes	Algebra II	95	0.500	0.500
1996-1997	2ND	Yes	Chemistry	95	0.500	0.500
1996-1997	2ND	Yes	Computer I	89	0.500	0.500
1996-1997	2ND	Yes	English 11	86	0.500	0.500
1996-1997	2ND	Yes	Geography	84	0.500	0.500
1996-1997	2ND	Yes	History/Writings Of Early	97	0.500	0.500
1996-1997	2ND	Yes	Spanish I	98	0.500	0.500

GPA: 3.5714   Total Credits: 3.500   3.500

Appendix B

The Presidents' Summit for America's Future - More than 4,000 people gathered in Philadelphia April 27-29, 1997 to celebrate a commitment to the nation's youth. The Presidents' Summit for America's Future drew a varied group – from United States presidents to religious and business leaders, young people, celebrities and just plain folks.

For more information about the Summit and how to get involved go to:
http://www.pointsoflight.org/programs/presidentssummit.html
or
http://www.americaspromise.org

04/28/90

These Scriptures are talking
about the return of the Lord
Jesus Christ, but they can
also refer to the vision you
have for your life which
is built on the Word of God.

Dare to dream and believe
God. The dream will come to
pass. No matter how difficult
the circumstances, God is
on your side. The victory is
yours through the Lord Jesus
Christ.

Habakkuk 2:3

For the Vision is yet for an appointed time, but at the end it shall speak, and not lie: though it tarry, wait for it; because it will surely come. it will not tarry

Hebrews 10:35-37

Cast not away therefore your Confidence, which hath great recompense of reward reward. For yet a little while and he that shall come will come. And he will not tarry

— Ardell Shockley
Denver, Co.

This scripture was given to me by a very sweet Christian lady. When she gave this to me it was at a period in my life when I did not understand what I was suppose to be doing to assist others…especially in helping youth obtaining lifelong education.

ABOUT THE AUTHOR

Rubye Graham-Emerson is a small town girl who has risen to every challenge life has presented her. Originally from McGehee, Arkansas, she was married and had moved to Gary, Indiana, by age 18. Rubye was a mother of two children when she began college. In the midst of earning her first college degree, her middle sister died, leaving three daughters. Rubye saw their need, recognized and seized her responsibility, and "adopted" her sister's children. Self-determination and inner strength helped her earn not only a Bachelor's degree but also a Master's degree (in Science Education with a major in Counseling Guidance Personnel Services) from Purdue University while owning and operating three state-licensed, full service infant, pre-school and kindergarten academies.

Currently an education representative at ITT Technical Institute, Rubye still finds time to "walk the walk" because she teaches education. She is a full-time student of Oral Roberts University, working on her Doctoral degree in Christian Education. She is active in her Sunday school class at First Assembly of God in North Little Rock where she continues to counsel and lead others in their quest to grow closer to our Lord and Savior Jesus Christ. She conducts educational workshops and a motivational guest speaker for organizations and groups.

Rubye is also an active member of the Pulaski County Republican Women Association as well as the secretary and a board member of the Arkansas Student Loan

Authority Board, to which Governor Mike Huckabee appointed her.

Rubye has been married to Leroy Emerson for more than 30 years and has two adult children, LeRoy W. Emerson and LaDana W. Emerson. She is also the grandmother of Dawnavan Noelani Emerson and LeRoi David Emerson.